BLACK HAWK

Frontier Warrior

by Joanne Oppenheim
illustrated by Hal Frenck

Troll Associates

Troll Associates, Mahwah, N.J.

Library of Congress Catalog Card Number: 78-18049
ISBN 0-89375-147-2

BLACK HAWK

Frontier Warrior

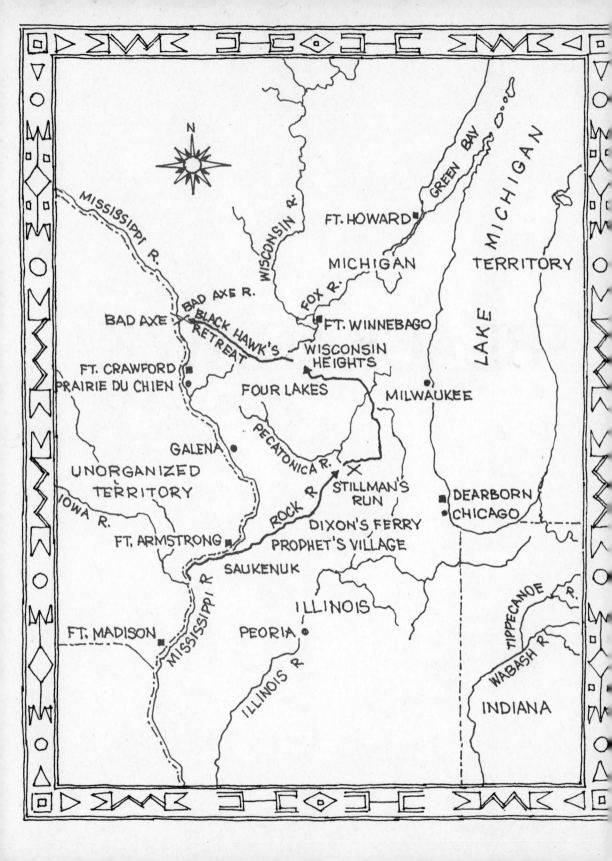

Black Hawk's sharp knife cut away the wet spring grass. With eager hands, he reached down into a deep hole.

"I have them!" he called to his father, Chief Pyesa.

One by one, the boy pulled many bark-covered packages out of the ground. They had been stored for safekeeping all winter.

"We shall have a fine feast!" said Black Hawk.

They carried the packages full of dried corn, beans, and crab apples toward their village.

"We must give thanks," said Pyesa, "for it is the Great Spirit who has given us our food and our land."

Women and children were already busy hoeing the wide fields outside the village of Saukenuk. This was the largest village of the Sauk Indians. One hundred lodges stood on the rich farmland between the Rock River and the Mississippi River in Illinois.

Every spring, the men of the tribe returned from the vast Sauk hunting grounds. They came back in canoes heavy with furs, telling many stories of great adventure.

Black Hawk listened as the braves told proudly
of their hunting deeds and their victories over
enemy tribes.

Some day, Black Hawk hoped that he, too,
would wear the feathers and paint of a War Chief.
His father, grandfather, and even his great-
grandfather had been Chiefs. Still, Black Hawk
knew he must prove his own strength first.

All through the late spring, Black Hawk ate well and played hard. He wore little more than beaded moccasins, a breechcloth, beads, and black paint on his face.

With the other Sauk boys, he raced, wrestled, and hunted. He played games of war too, for fighting was a way of life in his tribe. In time, the young Sauks would have to stand together against enemies of their people.

In the games, Black Hawk was fast on his feet and quick with his arrows. But he longed to prove his courage as a warrior.

"Games are for children," he told Pyesa. "I am ready to wear the feathers of a warrior!"

Pyesa smiled at his son's eagerness.

When the corn had been planted, the men
gathered in the council house. Black Hawk was
not old enough to sit with them. He knew that
soon the men would leave for the summer hunting. For weeks they would ride west, toward the
setting sun, to hunt buffalo and elk.

Again and again, he had asked Pyesa to take
him along. Always, the answer was the same:
"We will see, my son."

9

For fifteen summers, Black Hawk had gone to Rock Island with the women, children, and old men while the Sauk braves went on the summer hunt. The island was like a beautiful garden to his people. Here they gathered fruit, nuts, and berries. They fished and collected reeds for weaving mats. It was a peaceful time.

Still, Black Hawk longed for adventure.

One night, as he lay on his grass mat, Black Hawk heard the village crier calling, "Hunters make ready. We ride with the sunrise!"

He sighed impatiently. Why could he not go too?

Then he felt his father's hand on his shoulder. "Sleep, my son. Tomorrow you will ride with me!"

At last, Black Hawk saw with his own eyes the long cloud of dust that rose as the great herd of buffalo moved across the plains. His heart pounded as he rode beside his father.

"Take care, my son!" Pyesa called.

The earth thundered as the shaggy beasts were driven forward. Blindly, the buffalo ran straight toward the rocky walls of a canyon.

"Yeeoh!" the warriors cried, as the stampeding beasts fell to their death.

Tonight there would be a feast of buffalo ribs at the campfire, for now there would be good meat and fur robes to bring back to Saukenuk.

But Black Hawk's adventure for the day was not done. Just as the Sauks were giving thanks to the Great Spirit for their good hunt, a band of Osage warriors rode into the canyon.

Shrill war cries echoed. Bullets and arrows flew!

Black Hawk moved quickly. Suddenly, he was face to face with an Osage warrior. Clutching his hatchet, he raced toward his enemy and struck him down with one blow.

12

Few of the Osages lived to tell of that battle. Pyesa was proud of his young son. From that night on, Black Hawk could wear the feathers and paint of a warrior!

After six weeks, the hunters returned to Sau-kenuk. It was time for great feasts. Black Hawk proudly sang of his adventures at the council fire. He had seen battle. Now, he was a man among his people.

As the seasons passed, the Sauks and their brothers, the Fox Indians, followed the same paths. Black Hawk led them in many battles against any Osage, Sioux, or Cherokee warriors who dared to invade Sauk hunting grounds.

When Pyesa died, his people made young Black Hawk a Chief. There were many Chiefs among the Sauks, but Black Hawk was well known for his great courage and his ability to lead the warriors.

Black Hawk continued to follow the seasons as his father had done. Every year in the time of the falling leaves, he traveled down the Mississippi to trade with the Spanish in St. Louis.

For more than a hundred years, people from Spain, France, and England had come to the New World to trade. They brought blankets, axes, steel knives, and guns.

The Indians were glad to exchange their furs for these things. Most of all, they wanted guns and powder. Guns were best for hunting and for making war on enemy tribes.

18

But in 1804, when Black Hawk reached St. Louis, there was disturbing news. The Spanish were leaving. Now St. Louis belonged to the Americans.

Black Hawk was worried. For years, he had heard bad things about the Americans. They had taken land from his Indian brothers in the East. Black Hawk did not want their houses and fences near Saukenuk.

Black Hawk left St. Louis and brought the bad news to villages along the river.

Without Spanish gunpowder, his people would find it hard to hunt. Black Hawk took some of his men and traveled north. Maybe the English in Canada would give him powder.

While Black Hawk was in Canada, a small party of American soldiers came up the Mississippi River.

When they saw the soldiers' swords, some of the young Sauk warriors fired at the Americans. They were eager to do battle!

But the Chiefs did not want war. The Sauk and Fox tribes were used to fighting Indian enemies to keep them away from their hunting grounds, but they had no wish to fight the soldiers. So they called a council, and chose four Chiefs to go to St. Louis. They must make peace.

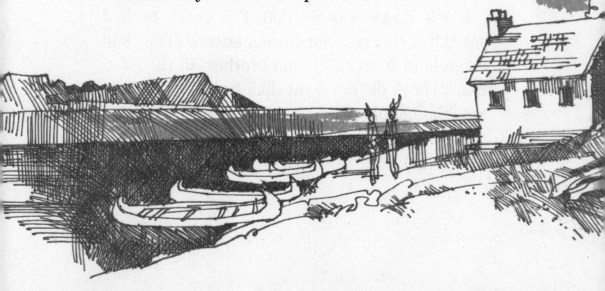

The four Chiefs had no trouble. The Americans even gave them gifts . . . they did not want war, either. But they did want land.

Before the Chiefs left St. Louis, they had put their marks on a piece of paper. They did not understand that they had signed away all the territories of the Sauk people.

Soon, boats full of soldiers came up the river. It was not long before the sound of their axes echoed over the land.

Angry and frightened, the Indians watched as the Americans chopped down trees to build a strong fort on Sauk land.

When Black Hawk returned from Canada, he heard what the Chiefs had done in St. Louis.

He was very angry!

"Such a treaty is worthless. They have tricked us. Four Chiefs do not own the land; four Chiefs cannot sell it. We will burn down the fort and drive the Long Knives off our land!"

Burning arrows flew over the fort. But as the Indians advanced, the soldiers loaded their cannons and fired.

Black Hawk drew back. He knew that arrows and small guns could not match the power of cannons.

Messengers were sent from the fort to Black Hawk's camp. The Americans told the Sauks that they did not want to fight. They said they had built the fort so they could trade with the Indians.

In the next few years, Black Hawk continued to trade for guns and powder with the English from Canada. The English were not generous, but they kept their promises.

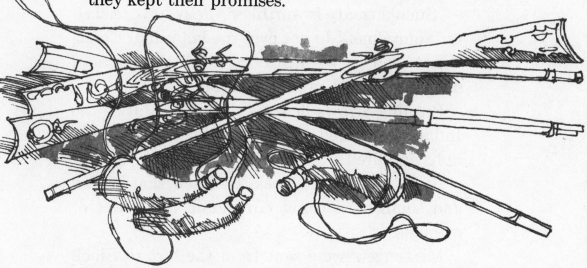

Then, far away from Black Hawk's campfire, trouble began to grow between England and America. On the high seas and in faraway ports, there was a new war, the War of 1812.

The American president, James Madison, sent word that he would give Black Hawk gunpowder if the Sauks would not help the English.

Black Hawk agreed. He did not want any part of the war. He wished only to be left alone.

26

When fall came, Black Hawk and his men went to the American fort. Soon, it would be time for the winter hunt.

Inside the fort, the soldiers gave the Sauks gifts of tobacco, food, and blankets . . . but no gunpowder.

Without gunpowder, how could they hunt? His people would starve!

28

Black Hawk was very angry. But when he
returned to his village, he found a welcome sur-
prise. An English trader had come secretly with
gifts, gunpowder, and good news!

The English, with the help of warriors of many
Indian Nations, were ready to make war on the
American forts to the north and east.

Black Hawk agreed to fight with the English.

For four long years, Black Hawk and hundreds of his warriors fought under the British flag. Sometimes it seemed as if the war would go on forever. Many times, the Sauks wondered why they were fighting a white man's war.

Finally, the war was over. The English had been defeated.

For Black Hawk and his people, it was the beginning of the end.

When Black Hawk returned to Saukenuk, things had changed. His rival, Keokuk, had been making agreements with the Americans about Sauk lands. In a council meeting, Keokuk said that the U.S. government had made him Supreme Chief of the Sauks and Foxes.

Black Hawk was enraged, and struck Keokuk.

But the Chief was not young any more. He felt in his heart that sadness and trouble would come to his people. The Americans had great might on their side.

So Black Hawk went with many other tribal Chiefs to St. Louis to smoke the pipe of peace with the Americans.

When they made their marks on a paper in May, 1816, the Chiefs thought they were signing a treaty of peace. Instead, they had promised to leave their Rock River country and move west of the Mississippi!

Later, Black Hawk said, "When I touched the goose quill to the treaty, I did not know that I consented to give away my village of Saukenuk."

Once again, the Indians had been tricked. Even before Black Hawk returned, soldiers were starting to build another fort—this time on Rock Island. Remembering the happy summer days he had spent on that beautiful island, the Chief's heart ached.

"The white men do not scalp the heads," he said. "They do worse. They poison the heart."

At the council fires, the Sauks no longer told proud tales of adventure. They spoke of trouble everywhere. Settlers were stealing the Indians' furs and spoiling their hunting grounds.

Sauk and Fox warriors had to raid Sioux hunting grounds for food. There were many small, bloody battles between the enemy tribes. Nearby settlers became terrified, and the government's demands for Black Hawk's people to move west increased.

In the village of Saukenuk, Keokuk urged the people to find new lands across the Mississippi.

"It is better to live in peace than to die of hunger," he said.

"You are a coward!" Black Hawk shouted. "The Great Spirit gave us this land to live upon. It belongs to the Great Spirit. We cannot sell it. We must not leave Saukenuk!"

Many braves turned away from Keokuk. Like Black Hawk, they would not leave their village.

Then, late one summer, Black Hawk and his men returned from the hunt to find settlers living in their village.

Black Hawk's grief was as great as his anger.

"They have burned down our ancient village and turned their horses into our growing corn!"

Now the Indians became truly a divided people. By 1830, Keokuk and many of the members of the Sauk and Fox tribes had moved across the Mississippi to a reservation in Iowa.

Black Hawk and his followers stayed in Saukenuk. But there was too much trouble between the settlers and the Indians. Word came that the government would send many troops to force the remaining Sauks off their own land.

Late in 1831, their hearts heavy, the Indians abandoned their lodges and their ripening corn to join their people in Iowa, far away from their home.

In Iowa, the Indians suffered a terrible winter. They did not have enough food. There was little shelter.

Black Hawk made up his mind. "We are left with the heart and heels of a rabbit in place of the courage and strength of the bear. There is only one thing we can do."

Then, in spite of Keokuk's opposition, Black Hawk and about four hundred of his warriors and their families decided to cross back into their land east of the Mississippi.

The return of so many Sauk and Fox warriors frightened the settlers.

Black Hawk said he had not come to make war, only to reclaim his people's land. But no one believed him.

As the word of his eastward journey spread through Illinois, the tension and fear grew almost unbearable. Soldiers were called up for battle. They began to march toward Black Hawk and his band. Something terrible was certain to happen.

Closer and closer the army marched. Finally, the first shots were fired. After that, there was no way to stop what was later to be called the Black Hawk War.

The Sauk and Fox were a proud and fierce people. They were used to the ways of war.

They fought bravely, but they had no food and few supplies. Not even their Indian allies would help them. Fresh American troops poured in daily. The Indians were being driven steadily westward across Wisconsin.

Knowing there was little hope for victory, Black Hawk finally sent three messengers carrying a flag of truce to a nearby enemy camp. But many of the volunteer soldiers were young and inexperienced. As the Indians rode toward them, the Americans shot them down.

With only about forty men, Black Hawk rushed furiously into the camp, frightening and confusing the Americans so badly that they ran in panic.

All summer long, the Indians and the soldiers hunted each other across the rolling prairies.

Black Hawk knew that it was a hopeless struggle. His warriors could not win against the endless lines of soldiers.

By August, the Indians had suffered terrible losses. When they reached the Bad Axe River, Black Hawk knew he must lead his band back across the Mississippi.

Exhausted and hungry, the men, women, and children moved toward the river. But before they could cross, the American steamboat *Warrior* opened fire. Caught between the army on land and the cannon and gunfire from the water, more than two hundred brave Sauks fell on that day.

Black Hawk escaped. But it was not long before he was forced to surrender at last to the
Americans.

Now he was a prisoner. He stood grimly on the
decks of the steamer that was to take him away
from the land of his people. He had seen almost
seventy summers on this land. Now he must leave
it forever.

With the defeat of Black Hawk, the United States gained possession of all the land from the Atlantic Ocean to the Mississippi River. Now nothing could stop the many wagons headed for the vast American West.

Chief Black Hawk waged war to try to prevent settlers from taking Indian lands. He was a patriot who fought hard to protect the right of his people to live on the land of their birth.

His words to his people and to the government agents at his surrender mark the end of an important era:

"Our sun is setting, and it will rise no more. Farewell to Black Hawk."